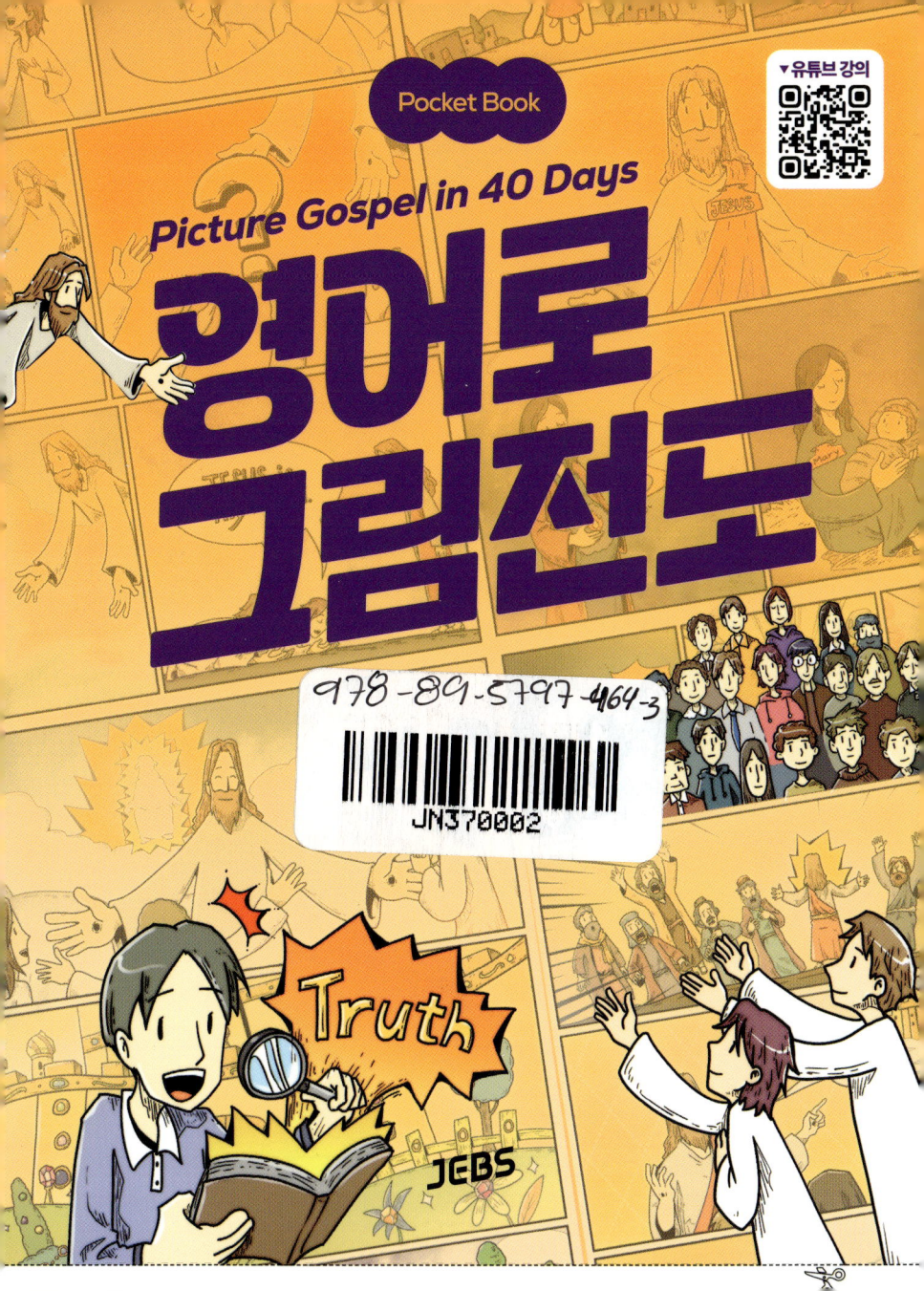

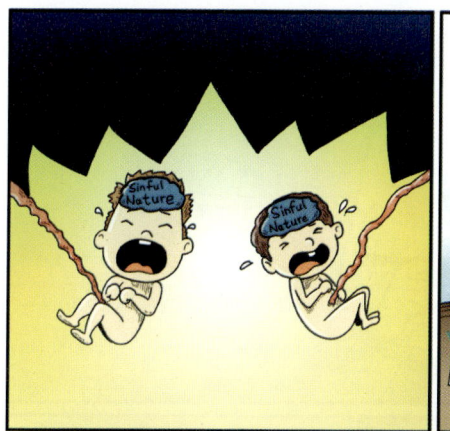

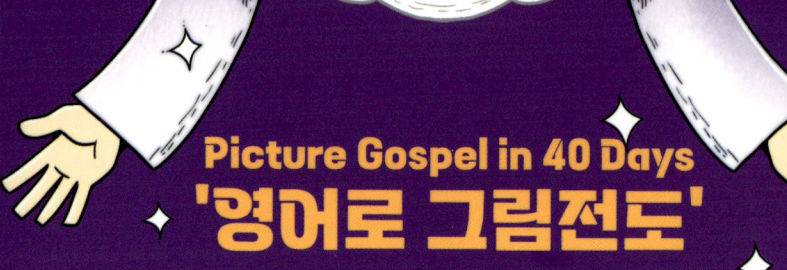

Picture Gospel in 40 Days
'영어로 그림전도'

How to Use

1

Take this pocket book with you wherever you go to evangelize.

2

Preach the gospel using the contents you recited through the Illustrative Mnemonic Technique.

3

Present the Picture Gospel book as a gift to help them remember the gospel afterward.

Pocket Book